World Stage Press
Verse from the Village

SUNSHINE

AND

CONCRETE

LYNDA LA ROSE

World Stage Press
Verse from the Village

World Stage Press
Verse from the Village

Sunshine and Concrete
Copyright © 2022 Lynda La Rose
ISBN: 978-1-952952-26-5

First Edition, 2022

Printed in the United States of America

Proofreading Edits by Laura Joy Phillips
Cover Design by Annie Cercone & Krystle May Statler
Layout Design by Ellie Woznica & Krystle May Statler

ACKNOWLEDGMENTS

OF COURSE, I must acknowledge family and friends first—very important. I'll do my best to not have this page sound like an Oscar speech.

Acknowledging Louie La Rose, my mother, and sisters Lisa and Laurie La Rose—love you all. Also my father, the late Dr. Arthur La Rose. His passing led to me writing poetry—very beautiful and unexpected to be sure. Love and shoutouts to my best and closest friends Anayansi Prado, Joy Alumit, Rivers Sears, William Irby, Gary Davidson, Ali De Vera, Stephanie Zamora, Sarah Spurr and all the ladies at my Sunday night poetry workshop. Also to other good friends I can't list here in the interest of time and space.

A huge thanks to my mentor, Joseph Culp, and the Walking Theatre Group. His hard work and dedication to his craft really inspires me to work—personally, I need the discipline. All the late nights and hours we spent at Electric Lodge in Venice, CA rehearsing for shows—were well worth it. The Walking in Your Shoes methodology and technique is something I still use to this very day. Love you, Joseph.

I want to give a shoutout to all the writing teachers that have helped me along the way (looking at you both, Terrie Silverman and Kelly Morgan). I always think of myself as a student, forever learning. Also, to the wonderful people at the Electric Lodge, 2017 Hollywood Fringe Festival, and Bootleg Theatre for bringing my solo show, *Summerfruit* into fruition. The ladies at the Los Angeles Women's Theatre Festival deserve equal credit as well. Of course, a huge thanks to the amazing SKY Palkowitz, my director, who wrote the foreword for this book.

The fabulous Overhead Projector reading that once existed at the former Onyx Café, in Los Feliz, deserves mad props as well (hate that the Onyx is gone—gentrification sucks). Milo Martin, Ben

Porter Lewis and all the poets who read there way back in the day— may the warm, glowing light of the Overhead Projector shine down on all of you!

Lastly, a very huge thanks to Hiram Sims, instructor Camari Carter-Hawkins, and fellow classmates in the Thursday Night Class at Community Literature Initiative! Season 8 is **_great!_** I couldn't have created this book without the wonderful people behind the CLI scenes—Nichole Gates, Annie Cercone, Ellie Woznica, Jerry Ayala, Kuahmel and all the other people there!

Sorry, I straight-up lied about not making these acknowledgments so Oscar speech-y (Mom, I tried not to make this so wordy). Except for Hemingway, most writers are verbose! Thanks to all and especially YOU, the reader, for being in my life!

Sincerely,
Lynda

dedicate this to the vowels between my teeth
dedicate this to the consonants under my tongue

the muse in my fingers gets all the praise.

TABLE OF CONTENTS

FOREWORD

SUNSHINE.

CONCRETE.

LANGUAGE.

I started writing poetry at 14 years old. It was a means of escape and expression, inspired both by the vast array of music I was exposed to in the 1980's, and my 9th grade Advanced Placement English teacher, who turned us on to some of the greatest literary works and ignited my passion for Shakespeare and reading aloud. Poetry, short stories, fiction, the classics—they all fascinated me.

At the same time, my being was urged forth to heed my calling and dedicate my life to entertaining and performing onstage. I began my serious training for the theatre. My respect for and wonderment of the English language, along with my discipline in the arts, led me to working with the top graduate conservatory for Shakespeare and classical theatre, The Professional Theatre Training Program at the University of Delaware, by the time I was 21. I went on to teach acting, discovered the world of solo artistry, and began writing my own works. I received my Master's Degree of Fine Arts from the University of Iowa, known for their new works and Advanced Playwriting program.

I have developed a large body of ongoing work that includes poetry, plays, and multidisciplinary performances, as well as a multitude of solo shows that I have created and performed around the United States and abroad since the early 1990s. My poetry has been published in magazines, national literary anthologies, books, articles, and online publications. I have scripted, created, directed, and performed nationwide, winning many poetry contests and awards. I've been producing, performing, hosting, and teaching in schools and theaters around the country for over three decades. I have developed and performed seven touring solo shows of my own, and have helped numerous others to hone their craft and present their own solo works.

Lynda approached me in 2016. I was speaking and conducting workshops for the Los Angeles Women's Theatre Festival (of which I am one of the Board of Directors) at our annual "Empowerment Day" for actors, theatre makers and solo artists. Lynda introduced herself and told me that she was a "performance poet" who secretly wanted to create a solo show to expand and showcase her work. She had a bunch of poems that she wanted to turn into a play.

I quickly became her dramaturg, her director, her producer, and her cheerleader. Lynda had a fresh perspective on the L.A. poetry scene, and now it was time to add characters, depth, dimension, and dialogue to her work. We spent two years developing her first solo show, *Summerfruit,* which we produced multiple times around Los Angeles, with much acclaim.

When The Pandemic hit in 2020, many theatre artists took to isolation. As a solo performance artist, director, and acting coach, it was devastating to think that it was no longer safe to step into a small theatre and perform in front of an intimate audience. I have been working with other multidisciplinary solo artists for many years, directing and producing, and assisting their creative visions to prepare them for full-length solo works for the stage, but quarantine changed all that. Now we are creating multimedia works for the world to see via the internet, working on Zoom, filming from home and using technology to bring these poems and stories onto the internet and across the world. We are making theatre, as was intended, with "all the world" as our stage.

I have directed and produced many experimental performance pieces and short films with students and clients worldwide. Lynda's ever-expansive world of words and her ability to shake up memories and stories and weave them into poetry and entertainment really lights my fire. She writes the poem, I vibe with her vision, I give her a bunch of filming instructions, and voila—a spoken word mission is ignited.

I do not think there is anyone more familiar with Lynda's massive body of consciousness-stirring poetics than myself. I have worked with her closely over the past six years, digging deeply into her words, dramaturging and developing her poetry into plays, and inspiring her to find new ways to recreate her spoken word and share it with the world. We have now produced over a dozen short films that speak to issues of pandemic, domestic violence, mental health, racism, the social status structure, heritage, and cultural identity.

Lynda inspires me to examine my own voice as a poet and writer, and to use the power of language to rattle the senses and progress the human condition forward. She is an important unknown author of our time, whose verses and visions represent and empower women, minorities, LGBTQ+ communities, and the Black Lives Matter movement, to name a few. Her work challenges us to question our own perceptions, and to expand our inherited paradigms when it comes to issues like racism, identity, and basic human rights.

Lynda is a fierce writer who is not afraid of vocalizing what others only think, but do not dare to say. Lynda's storytelling is a glimpse of uninhibited truth. She writes powerfully from her own personal experiences of growing up as the daughter of immigrants, a minority, and a woman of color in the heart of Los Angeles. She is a powerful voice of our times, and her work should be continued to be supported until it is circulated as required reading in the curriculum of our literary and educational system.

NOW, more than ever, it is time to come together as a people and respect our differences and celebrate our likenesses. It is more than our country that is at stake—it is OUR PLANET. As artists, it is our responsibility to create work that helps people understand, appreciate, influence thought and progress change. I enjoy working with artists who have something important to say, and I am finding great pleasure in guiding their visions and allowing the freedom of their voices to be heard in new ways and with new technology. Without fear, without boundaries, with passion, with activism, with urgency and artistry.

The expertise of powerful poetry lies not only in the scribing of words, but in the sounds and cadences of how to speak them, how to manipulate and tease the senses with presentation. Poetry is meant to be read aloud, thus the work of Ms. La Rose.

Lynda uses her personal stories to paint pictures of memories, and turns them into legible and audible experiences that unite us in the commonalities of being human so that we may share our experiences, ignite empowerment, accelerate visibility, create community, and revel in our evolution. Through her work we realize that when it all comes down to it, we are grappling with the same self-deprecating thoughts and behaviors, the same things that stop us, or make us shine. The similarities tie us together, and we find we are all One.

This is what the skillful craft of compiling words and dancing with the English language brings us. This is what you will find as you delve into the poems inherent in the first phase of published works by Lynda La Rose. This poet bares her soul, no holds barred, and tells it like it is. You will laugh, you will cry, you will ponder, you will visualize, and you will feel the sense of connection you have been searching for in her facility of weaving words, and the musicality of her language. I couldn't be more proud of what she has created, and am excited to see what the future holds in her insightful artistry.

Time is Now.

Now, when our planet's children have shifted their education to adapt to The Great Pandemic.

Now, when the English language has been so severely altered from its original form.

Now, when art and performance have been under threat of permanent shutdown.

Now, when the fabric of our nation has come undone, and its inherent racism has been revealed.

Now is the time that we need a good poem, a unique story, a force to be reckoned with.

Storytelling is a means of healing. A means of unification. Understanding. Compassion. Connection.

Poems that are touching. Poems that are angry. Poems that shake things up. Poems that inspire.

Rough around the edges and beautiful on the inside. Like Lynda. Like all of us. Like the world.

There is a sense of universal hope created here in *Sunshine and Concrete*.

May the sunshine light your face and warm your soul as you read.

Now is the time.

Time Is NOW.

Thank you, Lynda La Rose, for reminding us.

SKY PALKOWITZ is a Los Angeles-based, Avant-Garde Multimedia Performance Artist, Actor, Musician, Director, Producer, Educator, Speaker, and Activist who has been performing, teaching, and touring nationally for 30 years; who inspires, directs and produces multimedia works with California-based Minority and LGBTQ artists, and uses Theatrical Storytelling as a means of healing. For more info: www.DelusionalDiva.com. Lynda's ongoing collection of spoken word short films can be explored at www.YouTube.com/DelusionalDiva.

PREFACE

I NAMED THIS book "Sunshine and Concrete" because these poems can take you as high as the sun and smack you down on the asphalt at the same time. Recent times have been rough to be sure, but there was and is magic in between too.

There are poems in this book about school parties back in the day; swirling colored lights and a DJ holding it down at some L.A. nightclub out there; the magic of apricots; yellow curry in a coal black pot; pandemic and pain. There are poems about wanton political corruption, democracy with boots on the ground, strength and salvation. My female-identified Goddess muse weaves all the threads together.

all praises to the microphone
all praises...

NOTE FROM THE AUTHOR ON QR CODES

Throughout this book, you'll see QR codes to scan—those codes will link to YouTube videos of my poems. For those of you who don't know what a QR code looks like, here is a sample of one:

SCAN ME

Simply open up the QR app on your cell phone, scan the code and it will link to a video! Thanks and enjoy!

SUNSHINE

AND

CONCRETE

sunshine and concrete

under a grey orange sun
daisies grow near homeless campsites
riots break out while apricots ripen

under a grey orange sun
smog clouds a cerulean blue sky
syringes swim in white ocean waves

under a grey orange sun
democracy falls, rises, and falls again
sedition is just another wednesday

under a grey orange sun
quarantine is the great escape
taggers sign the city's name on billboard canvases

under a grey orange sun
L.A. is sandwiched in between sunshine and concrete
poems bloom under pandemic pressure

SCAN ME

prayer for lynda

all praises to the microphone
all praises
all praises to the microphone
all praises
all praises to the microphone
all praises

all praises to the microphone
for keeping my secrets
for listening to me when others would not
for amplifying my thoughts into poems
for loving me when no one else would

for setting me free
for setting me free

don't you know this mic is a priest and I'm the confessor
don't you know the coffeehouse table is my altar
don't you know that I'd lay down my life for the verb

mic, hear my prayer
o mic, hear my prayer

espresso machine whirring like a prayer wheel in the background
electric beats per minute of a poet spinning nouns
audience throwing themselves on the altar of the alphabet
mc leading us like a prophet to the promised land

word, set us free
word, set us free

in a war-filled world
we lay down arms for the word
when the money gets tight

we invest in the word
when there's no job to go to
we work for the word
when life beats us down
when hope slips through our fingers
when we have no choice
we bow to the word
we bow to the word
we bow to the word

and we bow to the mic
we praise you

amen

soul train kids

it was june 1975
end of the school year
summer was one big long recess for kids
time to put away the failed math tests and break out the earth wind
    and fire and ohiiiiiiiiiohhhhhh players
shove those books and desks aside
cause you can bet you last money it was gonna be a stone cold gas
    on the classroom floor
parrrrrrrrrt-tayyyyyy tiiiiimmmeeeee

don cornelius and shabby-doo had nothing on us fifth graders that
    was for damn sure
we could boogie on down
we could boogie on down
we could boogie on down with the best of them
in 1975 old school music was new school in our school
you had to float float on
float on float on
it was red hot un-huh reh he he hedddddddd
just make my funk the p-funk I wants to get funked up
do you remember the 21st night of september....
as far as us soul train kids were concerned we could forget that
    month for now
september sounded better when maurice white and philip bailey
    sang it
didn't want to see or think about those back-to-school clothes at
    sears yet

we were fueled by the red sugar rush of strawberry crush and
    hawaiian punch
there were all kinds of salty chips—laura scudders and lays and a
    big old bag of cheetos
we may have been late in turning in our homework
but we were not on the late freight with this real mother for yaaaaa

all of us got out of the teacher's single file line and in two sooooullll
    train lines
nancy did the football throwing a disco touchdown at the end of the
    line
alisha penguined her legs from side to side turning cool into cold
stephanie did the feel until she couldn't feel anything
mark huntley and marcellus popping and locking it up
roger richards roboting in the room
and as for me
as for me
as for me
I did that kinda dance I saw one of those glittery soul train divas did
    before the show was over and you heard that song
you know that song
doo doo doo dooo doooo doo doo let's get's it onnnnnn it's time to
    get down
one arm up the other arm swaying to a funked up disco beat
then I'd twirl and hop twirl and hop twirl hop twirl twirl hop twirl
    twirl hop down that line
didn't know the name of the dance
didn't know if the dance had a name
so what
didn't matter
you don't dance to the beat
the beat dances you
you don't dance to the beat

THE BEAT DANCES YOU

we danced and got down with our bad selves until the teacher
    brought in a big sheet cake that penny mcgee's mom bought for
    the party
we waited for that cake like the guest that got the party started
the teacher slowly sat the cake box on the table and opened the lid
as she opened it penny made a loud groaning noise
a big old hunk of cake was cut out
the "MER" from the word summer—gone

HAPPY SUM—the cake read now
there was only one person I knew who had the guts to do that
the principal of the school
if I were penny I'd be groaning too
cause I could not stand that woman
clearly the principal didn't know the principle of the thing

spinning one 33 after the other
from commodores' ("lady") to stevie's *innervisons* to marvin gaye's
    "I want you"
the soul train stayed in our station until it was time for our parents
    to pick us up after school

end-of-school partying
you could bet your last money
it was a
STONE
COLD
GAS

PEACE
LOVE
& SOOOOOUUUUULLLLLL!!!!!!!!!!!!

notes from the l.a. nightlife, 1988–2008

the words waited patiently in line and paid 10.00 cover charges
they were stamped on your left wrist as you entered lava lounge on
    sunset and la brea
they swung on a pole at the abbey on robertson
they twirled around with a pale skinny white guy on 80's night at
    some nameless dive on hollywood blvd
they danced bare-chested with t-shirts stuffed in their back pockets
    at revolver in WEHO
they caught a beat at the catch on pico
they grabbed your ass and smiled in your face while dancing at rage
    on santa monica even though they were gay
they ate the cheap cardboard pizza served every friday night at the
    old school joint on cahuenga whose name you can't remember
    now

upload the image of the bouncers laying out the drunk guy in the
    parking lot at 2am
they laid him out like a dead log
we stepped over him one foot after the other

burn the confused look of the fool on the stinging end of a girl's slap
    at the bar

save the oceans of sweat gushing from your friend jill's body down
    to her thirsty bustier as her body shook on the dance floor

don't delete these memories from your pen

in the back of the clubs you took notes with your eyes
and then you took a club kid's vow to worship at the altar of the dj
    spinning one prayer after the other
savor those words like you sipped the nine-dollar midori sour in
    your hand

in that moment you were toulouse-lautrec in your own moulin rouge
you used swirling lights as your palette

you are making good on your promise ten to thirty years later to
    write about night dwellers on an l.a. dancefloor

you witnessed *we are family* broken down in dance moves
you observed *how soon is now* expressed in body rhythm
you surveyed *suavemente* and your feet felt compelled to dance to
    their own cha-cha
you plugged into EDM's electric beats sung by lisa shaw
you humped with humpty doing *the humpty dance*

you took an oath to see the club
hear the club
taste the club
smell the club
touch the club

the words will dance themselves when it's time

SCAN ME

Red States vs. Blue States: Secession 2020

Red states, we want a secession from you!
Let's face it—we're going in two different latitudes and longitudes!
Your silent majority spoke loudly with your votes for trump!
Clearly you've made your choice and it isn't US!

We're cutting off all state lines with you!
You'll hear from my surveyor in the morning!
We're packing our things—
sunshine,
the beach,
the entertainment industry,
the empire state building,
the Statue of Liberty,
people of all orientations and gender identities plus anti-racism.
You can have the 2nd Amendment, Confederate statues, Kid Rock
    and Scott Baio!
Joanie doesn't love Chachi anymore!

Don't try to contact us for goods or taxation!
Whatever resources we brought to our 240+ year annexation we
    will take with us!

We really do wish you all the best.
Don't take it personally.
It's not US—
it's blue!

SCAN ME

when he leaves

when he leaves
block his Twitter
his number
his email
his access to Black, Brown, Asian, LGBTQ+, Non-Binary, and
    Indigenous people

when he leaves
convert his tanning bed into a wind turbine
fake sun gives you cancer anyway not wind
when he leaves
toss out the sharpie that doctored the hurricane map
the cognitive exam that one of his aides took for him and passed
the upside-down bible he gassed people to hold
the mask he never wore during the 'rona
the empty cans of goya beans
the snorted crumbs of sudafed from the drawer of the resolute desk
he was the virus we needed to disinfect ourselves from all along
we are resolute to move on from him

jettison the mikes
the stephens
the seans
the sarahs
the kellyannes
the kayleighs
that big blob of greasy mayo bill barr
we're tired of white people flying around whitely in the white house

we're putting putin in the rearview
we're reclaiming our space from ivanka and jared
we're dunking don jr. in the deepest part of the ocean
we're kicking eric to the curb while we're at it
'cause melania, we really don't care, do you?

we're tossing everyone out
but Mary and Barron can stay
they're our Caucasian allies now

when he leaves
let him chill in sing sing or san quentin
he finally got his wall after all
let him make it great behind bars!

you're special [A SONG]

hey mr. white riot
I'm singing a song
thought you could take votes over
but I guess you were wrong

black and brown power
kept you in check
don't even try it next time
or havoc we'll *"wreck"*

[CHORUS]
trump loves you, white boy
you're special
you're special
trump loves you, white boy
you're special
you're special

busting up the capitol
you're going to jail
you thought sedition was cool
it's an epic fail

thought you would win
but democracy's back
you messed up big time
with your vicious attack

[CHORUS]
trump loves you, white boy
you're special
you're special
trump loves you, white boy
you're special

you're special

done with you now
I'm shaking the spot
you should have stayed home
now you're gonna get caught

but you're special, jail bird
you're special
you're special
you're special, jail bird
you're special
you're special

[CHORUS (2x)]
trump loves you, white boy
you're special
you're special
trump loves you, white boy
you're special
you're special

mourning news

and in San Diego, the caravan is 20 miles away
and in Parkland, I can almost hear the gunshots
and in L.A., a nurse is living in her car
and in D.C., it's day 23 of the shutdown

another young brother's life never mattered to a cop in Baltimore
living while Black gets you killed
living while Black gets you killed
living while Black gets you killed

in Charlottesville, tiki-torch whites are making America dark again
chanting you will not replace us
you will not replace us
you will not replace us

trump raped yet another Woman
trump raped yet another Woman
trump raped yet another Woman

in the shadows Putin's watching the nation fall one vote at a time

Puerto Rico is in darkness
I still can't drink the water in Flint

I see a migrant dad and his daughter dead face down in the Rio
    Grande
I hear children in cages crying for their parents
I taste tears streaming down my face watching 24-hour news cycles
I'm in mourning over morning news

poets write the soul of the nation but I alone cannot fix this
do you think I can band-aid this country with a few well-placed
    syllables and consonants?
do you think my words can stop COVID-19 from killing us all?

do you really think I can reunite immigrant children with their
   parents?
no one can replace them
no one can replace them
no one can replace them

I am stretched five thousand miles between Alaska and Maine
one hurricane after another is coming
earth is under water and we can't pay the mortgage
america is in the ICU bleeding out
poets write the soul of the nation
I alone cannot fix this

we write the soul of the nation but we aren't firefighters
we write the soul of the nation but we aren't superheroes

I alone cannot fix this
this is not an alternative fact

america come with me
grab a piece of paper and write a better future
get out your laptops and get us out of this mess
go to a government near you and speak your truth like you're
   rocking the mic
write the ending for our poem like your pen is on fire

only WE can write this

SCAN ME

the time is NOW

the time is now
the time is now
motherlovers let me tell you
the time is now

virus annihilates
time is now

black lives terminate
time is now

whites full of hate
time is now

lack of jobs agitate
time is now

motherlovers
let me tell you
the time is now

time to march in the street
it is now
mask it up don't retreat
it is now
politicians unseat
it is now
it is now

IT
IS
NOW

so, what are you gonna do???
the time is now

if not you, then who?
the time is now
dump a white man statue?
the time is now

let's create a love coup!
the time is now
the time is now
the time is now

motherlovers
let
me
tell
you

the

time

is

NOW!

plagued

one one thousand—two one thousand
virus hiding under my nails

three one thousand—four one thousand
my hands are scared of you

five one thousand—six one thousand
won't let it take me

seven one thousand—eight one thousand
it could hide if I let it

nine one thousand—ten one thousand
knuckle it down

eleven one thousand—twelve one thousand
drown it in hot water

thirteen one thousand—fourteen one thousand
you are the death snowflake

fifteen one thousand
my black skin saved by white soap

sixteen one thousand
seventeen one thousand
scrub the color out of me
eighteen one thousand
please don't kill me
nineteen one thousand
I don't want to die
twenty one thousand
please let me live
please let me live

SUNSHINE AND CONCRETE

please

let

me...

SCAN ME

Red is Beautiful

in summer me and my sisters lisa and laurie would take mom's old
    faded-out yellow bedspread and lay it on the brown lawn under
    the peach tree
we'd lie out in the sun pretending to be white girls getting a tan
look at how fast I tan lisa would say flipping her hair back and forth
    and back and forth
like a blonde woman in a breck shampoo commercial
laurie and I rolling and laughing hysterically on the lawn
but secretly I would push my hair back at the top of my forehead
I had blonde hair too just like those women on tv
I could be white around the forehead
besides mom told us the other day that our great great grandfather
    was from scotland
all of us sisters could be white if we wanted to

but we were black
and black was beautiful like the revolutionary chant we heard on
    the tv and the street all the time
black was bold and beyond basic
we would never be blonde like our barbie dolls in our barbie country
    camper that we all bought together with our collective allowance
they had plastic bodies and blonde plastic hair
black is beautiful
black is beautiful
black is beautiful

AND IT JUST DON'T CRACK

yellow blanket with black girls changing color in the noonday sun
turning reddish like the peach on the top branch
RED IS BEAUTIFUL
RED IS BEAUTIFUL
RED IS BEAUTIFUL
and it just don't crack

SCAN ME

Apricots for Mom

there is an old picture we have of mom eating an apricot in the
    backyard
she loved apricots just as much as I do
she'd get the rusted old fruit picker sitting near the side of the house
    and pick the best pieces
pick those apricots faster than the birds and the boys did
she would wash and peel them
put them in a pot
and transform them into a sweet jam

mom's jam was better than any snickers bar I got from the liquor
    store up the street
liquid gold in a jar
no need to unwrap
just spread it on toast
close your eyes
and let the sweetness seep through the pores of your skin...

Excerpts from *Summerfruit*
A Solo Poetry/Spoken Word Play

PHOTO CREDITS: TERENCE MAY AND JOY ALUMIT

SUNSHINE AND CONCRETE

A Brief History of *Summerfruit*

I WROTE AND performed my solo poetry/spoken word show, *Summerfruit* in 2007. I'd never written a solo show before and, to my amazement, the show was a success! I took over ten years to rewrite and revise the script and to learn about acting in the Walking Theatre Group in Venice, CA, under the careful guidance of Joseph Culp, the group's founder. In 2016, I met my future director SKY Palkowitz, who dramaturged the script (it was just a bunch of poems back then—no stage directions at all). The show premiered in the 2017 Hollywood Fringe Festival—we had two oversold nights and standing ovations on both nights! In 2018, SKY and I took Summerfruit to the Bootleg Theater's "Solo Queens Fest", where it was well received! The show tells the story of a young girl ripening into womanhood through various summers of her life, looking for love in family, her neighborhood, food, men, sexuality, the muse, and apricots. I've included excerpts from the show.

SCENE 1 – "SOUL CHILD IN THE 70's"

SCATTERED PROPS AND COSTUME PIECES PLACED NEAR
CHAIR STAGE RIGHT CENTER, MIC STAND DOWNSTAGE LEFT
AND BLOCK UPSTAGE LEFT

STAGE IS IN COMPLETE DARKNESS –

LIGHT CUE 1 – SINGLE LIGHT COMES UP ON A YOUNG GIRL
DOWNSTAGE CENTER AS

SOUND CUE 1 – DRUMS BEATING

HOMELESS WOMAN AGE 11

Summertime, circa 1970, 71, 72, 75, 77—so
what—it doesn't matter!!!! Somewhere in
Midtown LA there are two streets that
intersect, Ogden Drive and Saturn Street.

SOUND OF DRUMS BEGIN TO FADE OUT

Somewhere in the middle of town between the
auto body and the barbershops, the Stop
N Go and Safeway, Mickey D's and Canton
Chef and those red tiled roofed houses
with magnolia trees and burned out lawns
there's a corner house—and that corner
house has seen a lot!

SOUND OUT

The corner house has seen white folks flying
out of the neighborhood and Black folks
flying in to nest. It's tasted the warm
sweet juice of a ripened apricot fallen
from the tree in the backyard. It's felt
the fast rubber burn of boys on banana
seat bikes. It's heard parents screaming
at each other late at night. It's held

the knees of gangbangers at a midnight
cop bust. Smelled the rich amber taste of
curry simmering in a coal-black skillet
on the stove.
This is our house. Somewhere between the
gray orange sun and a hot pavement, in
between springtime and fall.
There are dramas within and without and the
corner house has seen all.

*(The young girl takes apricot from pocket and
examines it- fades into black.)*

LIGHT CUE 2 - lights up on stage, bright, daytime

SCENE 2 - PRESENT DAY - "HOMELESS"

*(HOMELESS WOMAN is agitated and pissed off. PUTTING
ON PONCHO as she begins)*

HOMELESS WOMAN
was in my old house on Ogden and Saturn
walked around each room-didn't recognize
    anything
chairs and tables and beds not mine
ran to the dining room and saw a family I
    didn't recognize
all smiles-laughing and talking

*(HOMELESS WOMAN mimes a broom, sweeping first, then
brandishing it like a spear, holds it threateningly.)*

I yelled LEAVE but they couldn't hear me
I took a rake and smashed the window
the dream pushed me out of bed and woke me
    up

*(HOMELESS WOMAN sings a few lyrics from 70's song
"Backstabbers":)*

> "they smile in your face
> all the time they want to take your place
> the backstabbers
> backstabbers..."

*(HOMELESS WOMAN moves a prop or two back and forth
from the same spots. She twirls her wrists and
fingers while she speaks.)*

> I had a boyfriend, house, money–what
> happened to them?
> need to go back home–is it still alive?
> where are the brown-skinned kids having a
> cool off in the sprinklers???
> can I feel my bare feet in the green grass
> again?
> something is not right
> some white lady's riding her 10 speed down
> Ogden Drive
> there's a white man jogging out of a house
> half a block down
> see a curly-headed-blonde girl bouncing out
> of our old house
> no more meaty meat burgers on Fairfax and
> Pico
> cheesy not greasy pizza is now RAW FOOD
> DAILY
> should be happy I'm walking on my home turf
> my feet know every pebble and stone of this
> concrete pavement
> every blade of grass has my fingerprints on
> them
> the sidewalk is angry
> times are changing and I don't know what to
> feel

(HOMELESS WOMAN sings lyrics from "I Wish")

    I wish those days could come back once more
    Why did those days ev-er have to go
    I wish those days could come back once more
    Why did those days ev-er have to go
    Cause I love them so

(HOMELESS WOMAN picks up Archie comic book, flipping through and examining it.)

    over 40 summers ago white people lived here
    after the riots in '65, Blacks moved in
    whites moved out
    even for them now it's getting a little too
        expensive in Brentwood or Santa Monica
    now they're pushing us out!

(HOMELESS WOMAN throws Archie comic books across the stage. She picks her notebook and pen and starts writing in Archie comic book.)

    as she wrote
    she saw a glimmer of light
    photosynthesis redefined
    colors refracted in rainbow hues
    she saw atoms spinning forever
    making things matter
    the cellular truth in constant division and
        refinement
    where's tumbleweed?
    where's brothaman?
    where is that bored girl in the hot house?
    lived in L.A. my whole life
    where is my home???
    the backyard?
    the apricot tree?

(HOMELESS WOMAN rips off camouflage poncho and transforms into young girl again, wearing orange shirt and white drawstring pants. She runs downstage center, mesmerized by an apricot tree in her backyard.)

SCENE 3 - 1970's - "SUMMER'S INTRO"

HOMELESS WOMAN AGE 11
(seeing giant tree in front of her)

    hold a piece of summer in my hands
    roll it in between my fingers and thumb then
        bite it
    juice moistens my lips
    lick the sun off my fingers one by one
    can climb up to the top branch and get the
        sweetest fruit
    hope the birds haven't pecked it out

(She mimes climbing the apricot tree.)

    can smell everything—the grass, dog crap,
        asphalt, green leaves, smell of mom's
        curry on the stove

(over her shoulder, imitating her mother)

    "Lynda!!! Dinner!!!"
    I climb, stick my tongue out, try to catch
        some sun
    all I get is some gray L.A. smog that stings
        and burns

(She stops climbing the tree and looks down and out—holds a branch and rocks back and forth a little on tiptoes.)

now standing on a huge branch,
see things from a great height
from up here see tumbleweed and his boys
    strolling by our fence
every summer they always hop it and steal
    the apricots;
birds and those boys always know where the
    best apricots are on the tree,
they steal and fly away
below hear parents yelling in the bedroom

MOM

(over shoulder)

where the hell were you last night?
DAD
(over shoulder)

get off my back

MOM

(over shoulder)

I smell some woman's perfume on your clothes-
    who is she???

*(She takes a beat and quickly climbs up the tree
like she's running away from the yelling.)*

HOMELESS WOMAN AGE 11
climb
through summer clouds
blue sky
hot pavement
big afro-ed boys
through words thrown by mom and dad in anger
    that stick on hot clammy walls climb

(She stops climbing, picks an apricot, and twirls it around in her hand.)

I keep climbing
pick an apricot
something is moving, crawling up and down
   my hand then the middle of my elbow
one ant then two ants then twelve then 50
an apricot murdered first by a careless bird,
   then by ants—
throw apricot to the ground and the small
   black bodies surround and swallow the
   fruit

(She mimes throwing apricot to the ground...She climbs, sees an apricot on the tree, holds it in her hand, twirls it around, has not picked it yet.)

get to the top of the tree, see another one,
a yellowish face smiling-blushing-reddish
   orange,
so pretty, so perfect—
do I pick it or let it be?
I could let it alone but it will ripen and
   fall to the ground
ants will get it and birds will peck it to
   death
I could throw it over the fence but those
   boys will grab and eat it up
I could eat it, but then it would be gone

(She clutches apricot in her hands—her body looks unsteady and looks like she may fall.)

I'm holding tighter, afraid I'll crush it
my feet are slipping on this branch—

the tighter I hold, the more I kill it
if I let go, I'll fall

LIGHTS BEGIN TO FADE

I can't let go
I can't let go
I can't let go

SCENE 5 - 1970's - "TUMBLEWEED"

(Young girl mimes holding a hose, watering the lawn—she's standing near the backyard fence—she walks to the fence and peeks outside every so often.)

HOMELESS WOMAN AGE 11

Tumbleweed was 14 and so much older than I
    was
he had a honey-blonde 'fro as big as a
    spinning desert bush
didn't know what his real name was
he had honey-colored skin to match
a cake cutter comb falling off the back of
    his head, making him look like a walking
    question mark
winter or summer he always wore that same old
    down jacket with the sleeveless t-shirt
khaki pants a little baggy in the crotch
    and black croker sax shoes on his feet

(She imitates Tumbleweed's crip walk.)

Tumbleweed didn't just walk the sidewalk
    he rolled on it
rolled on it like a concrete wave
doing that hop step slide hop step slide

hop step slide of his ca-rip walk
there was no breeze on a humid July on my
    street
that didn't matter cause that boy glided up
    and down Ogden
and all I wanted to do was get a close whiff
    of his afro sheen
sometimes I'd imagine Tumbleweed buying me
    pop rocks, orange soda
and wacky packs from Okay Liquor store down
    on Pico Blvd.

(She mimes picking a dandelion from lawn.)

picking a dandelion from some neighbor's
    lawn and gently handing it to me one time
    he actually spoke to me
he said "what's up girl" as he rode his bike
    past our front lawn
wonder what would it'd be like to taste the
    orange soda from your lips or even meet
    your mom—
the only person who didn't like him was my
    mom
sucking her teeth and calling him names
    like "orangutang" in her sing-songy,
    West Indian accent

(She runs downstage center to fence.)

I was watering the lawn in the backyard
    when I saw him
I ran to the fence and my eyes followed
    him as he strolled up Saturn with his
    friends Riley and Le Beau

*(She walks in a circle and mimes TUMBLEWEED eating
polly seeds.)*

they cracked one polly seed after the other
shells of polly seeds left in their wake
then mom yelled out the window and caught
   me

MOM

stop staring at that boy
I don't want him looking inside here
he steals apricots
who knows what else he could steal??

HOMELESS WOMAN AGE 11

as he got closer to our backyard I threw the
   hose down on the lawn and hid behind the
   avocado tree

(She runs upstage center and acts likes she's hiding.)

didn't want mom catching me
if tumbleweed sees me he could call me fat

(She peeks out from her "hiding place.")

they stood near the fence and the smell of
   warm apricots filled their nostrils with
   sensual delight and an urge to steal

(HOMELESS WOMAN AGE 11 runs downstage center, turning into TUMBLEWEED—she holds up her fist like a Black power symbol.)

afro-disiac to the core!

(TUMBLEWEED climbs up the fence and hops up to the apricot tree.)

Tumbleweed climbed up the fence one croker
    sack, then next
leaped up to the top branch and grabbed
    something wet and juicy

TUMBLEWEED

*(He talks over his shoulder to his boys, mimicking
eating pussy, using his tongue.)*

funny how ripe apricots is like pussaay but
    only on a tree!

HOMELESS WOMAN AGE 11
I heard him say to riley over his shoulder!

TUMBLEWEED
soft, fuzzy and juicy as hell!

(He throws an apricot to one of his boys.)

here, catch!
grab one little piece, then the next!
that's how you gotta treat them broads most
    of the time!
just take it and get the hell out!

HOMELESS WOMAN AGE 11
all this time I was looking at him from
    behind the tree
he may have been a thief but it was my
    backyard he was stealing from—
a weird sort of blessing and an honor!
as Tumbleweed stuffed the last apricot in
    his jacket
Mom came out with her broom and swept him
    out of there!

(She marches stage left, transforming into MOM—mimes picking up broom and dustpan, marches downstage center and waves broom and dustpan in the air as a warning to Tumbleweed, shooing him away.)

MOM
(yelling to TUMBLEWEED)

GET THE HELL OUT OF HERE!!!!

(MOM drops broom and dustpan and transforms into TUMBLEWEED, running in place.)

HOMELESS WOMAN AGE 11
Tumbleweed leaped out of the backyard so fast a croker sax almost fell off his foot!

TUMBLEWEED
(yelling to MOM)

"YOU CRAZY ASS CRAZY BITCH, I'M GONNA GET YOU!"

HOMELESS WOMAN AGE 11
he said over his shoulder while he and his boys booked on out of there!!!

(TUMBLEWEED flips bird to audience/MOM and yells "Uhhh! TUMBLEWEED crouches down and puts hands on knees, transforming back into young girl-SHE bounces a little on her heels as she watches the tv.)

HOMELESS WOMAN AGE 11
later on that evening in mom and dad's bedroom

watching love american style...truer
than the red white and bluuuuuueee...

(She suddenly moves back like she's been hit by a
huge tidal wave, waving her arms with the shock.)

BAM!!!! CRASH!!!!!

(She moves cautiously and looks like she's examining
something dangerous on the floor—picks up broom and
dustpan and starts sweeping cautiously.)

glass all over the bed
glass on the floor
on mom's nightstand
our old rusted rake smashed through the
    window pane

(She moves broom handle like she's smashing
something.)

(She looks out to the audience like she's looking
through a window.)

I looked through the window and saw someone
    running up Saturn
he had a honey-blonde 'fro

(She sweeps broken glass into dustpan—looks out
into audience.)

but maybe it wasn't him
there were boys with him that looked like
    Riley and Le Beau from the back
maybe it was some other guys
still
I do love him

LIGHTS BEGIN TO FADE

Tumbleweed!
Tumbleweed!!
Tumbleweed!!!

(She looks out into audience again searching for Tumbleweed.)

SCENE 6 - 1970's - "DAD'S OFFICE"

(A young girl is in dad's office in summertime.)

always in summer I would work at dad's office

right in the middle of bustling smoggy western avenue near venice near McDonalds and Fatburger-

edge of the hood but not quite the hood

I loved Dad as Dr. La Rose, OB/GYN

ushering Black babies into the world both planned and unplanned

administering to a patient high on some drug or another

she may or may not have been loyal to friends or family but she was always loyal to Doctor

she'd make sure to show up on time to keep her appointment cause the baby was due in a few weeks

I'm sure there must have been something magical about listening to a baby's undersea heart in a pregnant woman's belly

a life round and full just like a woman's

patients would be sitting all around that vinyl blue plastic couch of his

(She mimes being an impatient patient, squirming in her chair.)

>   all that heat generating from sitting there for an hour or two would make their thighs all sticky and wet
>
>   acting like impatient kids waiting for their mom to pick them up making all kinds of noise wanting to see doctor
>
>   "I gotta see Dr. La Rose!
>
>   Where is Doctor????"

(She transforms into ERNESTINE the receptionist— mimes picking up phone receiver.)

>   trying to work the last nerves of Ernestine the receptionist
>
>   she'd take a long drag from the Kool cigarette hanging out from her lip
>
>   take a long sip from the 9th Pepsi she had that morning

(She hangs up phone receiver—mimes smoking a cigarette and drinking Pepsi.)

ERNESTINE
(yelling over shoulder)

>   you know, y'all need to hush!
>   Doctor is coming-just hush!

(She transforms into an impatient patient sitting in chair, looking prissy and people pleasing.)

and then when he'd finally arrive
they'd get real quiet and sweet like they
   were waiting for only five minutes
Dad not only had bedside manner but waiting
   room manner too
somehow to me it was kind of an honor to
   change the tissue paper on the tables in
   the examining rooms or file stuff in the
   patients' charts
I'm like my dad too, you know, even though
   I may not want to be a doctor-
these hands can heal
even though I'm 11 and too young to operate
   on anyone-
my hands make a difference in a small way
so cool!
when it was lunchtime Reverend Shepard would
   come to the office,
small lightskin little man in a black suit
   and porkpie hat

(She mimes putting on a hat with a brim.)

didn't know where his church was but we
   always called him Reverend
he'd always bring us some Big Macs or
   sometimes even a Fatburger from down the
   street

REVEREND

Afternoon Miss Ernestine, Afternoon Miss
   Laverne, and hello Miss lovely little
   Lynda. Got you each a little something
   something for you in my Big Mac sack!

HOMELESS WOMAN AGE 11

during lunchtime dad would pass out on that
old olive green couch of his snoring
like a buzz saw

(She transforms into LAVERNE—shivering and shuffling
papers from left to right—writing things down)

annoying the hell out of Laverne, the
bookkeeper who'd always be shivering and
turning up the heat in the office even
though it was 90 degrees outside

LAVERNE

(under her breath)
Don't know why that man doesn't sleep at
his own house.
Ooooh, it's so cold in here. I'm turning up
the heat!!

HOMELESS WOMAN AGE 11

and then I understood
this was Dad's house
a home without the underwear thrown on the
floor or a Lakers game blaring on the TV,
he took care of all those women who needed
him just like a father would,
this was his home
and I was safe

SCENE 7 - 1970s - "SECOND HOME"

HOMELESS WOMAN AGE 11

(standing downstage center)
dad found a second home besides the green
couch in his office
smooth brown arms (not his wife's) slowly
welcomed him in—

the younger a woman is the faster she can
   run
so the other woman ran easily into dad's
   arms
he wasn't aware they were open until he
   felt her head on his chest
middle of his life
summer and a young woman's arms may never
   come again...
and my mother's arms were left alone with
   the weight of the situation
and so the wars in our house began–
why does anger always smell like rancid
   meat?

Yellow off the Bone

mom's curry in summertime
smell of earth and spice in a black coal pot....

I want something to remember yellow by
like the pot sitting on mom's stove remembers yellow
the pot remembers her gold braceleted hands as they cut pieces of
    chicken leg by wing by thigh
along with the celery, tomato, and onion
as the chicken would simmer it would surrender to color

after my mother cooked the curry,
yellow would hang on the walls
sit on the furniture
breathe in the spaces between our fingers and toes
and the pot would bleed yellow for days

as mom's hands stirred the curry, they remembered a time when
    she was a young girl in St. Vincent
her mother's hands guided hers to stir
they remember the strong smell of mustard lingering in the hot
    humid air
the melt of amber in her mouth

and one day the pot will be mine
one day I will conjure curry in a black midnight pot like my mother
    and her mother before her
one day I will coax yellow to fall off the bone
one day I will become yellow earth

SCAN ME

insurrection is instagrammable

her private plane parted the burning white clouds
she descended the golden cessna and stood in front of the lynched
    Capitol Building
she fired up her IG app on her phone faster than she could hashtag
    #revolution
in a bear sprayed haze she took a selfie and filtered clarendon for
    ethics and lark for conscience
texas blonde smile on her red lips holding up a french manicured
    peace sign
she posted a story on her sedition profile
her caption was "I'm a nice person supporting my president"
    #patriotismismybrand

FBI is one of her followers now
will she get a like or a pardon?

SCAN ME

breyonna's behalf

do me a favor
pretty please while you're at it
send them to jail now

2020 in 5-7-5

'rona. george. ahmaud.
trump's taxes and woodward's tapes.
biden, fix this mess!

we're over it

so done with karens!
they'll be the death of us all!
white privilege, time's up!

Post-Election Chill Out

So glad it's over!
Biden won with Kamala!
Let us get to work!

Proud Boy Mandate

White boys with guns
would make trump God if they could!
Stand back and stand by!

Virus Victory

I'm alive, dammit!
Slipped out of the 'rona's grasp!
My Black life matters!

a post-election memo to trump's lawyers

recount all those votes!
break the news to him gently!
two plus two is four!

Black Folks to America's Rescue in 2020 (Once More!)

if it weren't for us
there would be no votes for him!
saved it once again!

lone 'rona warrior

where's everybody?
we have hit the second wave!
can't do this alone!

trump's assertion aka some fishy ballots

"thrown in a river!"
look, we pulled them out for you!
votes cast for biden!

Minor Adjustments to the 2020 Turkey Day Holiday

Thanksgiving's on Zoom.
Come on now, what's the big deal?
Stuffing's in the chat!

Merry Chrisma-Kwan-COVID-kah!

Holidays during
pandemic are rough but still
worth celebrating!

45's early x-mas gift

so he pardoned flynn.
manafort is surely next.
get in line, bad guys!

My Virus Disinfecting Battle Cry

"Wake up–time to die!"
Stole that line from Blade Runner!
It's 'rona or me!

give me liberty...

did not wear a mask
so what was the cause of death?
his "freedom," of course!

the upside of the pandemic

the good news is that
white people don't touch my hair.
negritude unharmed.

January 20th Can't Come Soon Enough

Taking a ringside
seat for the U.S. Marshals
to toss his ass out!

trump's going away party

they sang in the streets,
"you about to lose your job!"
the countdown starts **_NOW!_**

284,000 Virus Homicides (as of 12/8/2020)

For the love of God
please wear a damn mask, people!
Should not have to beg!

trump's election lawsuits:
2016 mission accomplished

winning at losing!
a campaign promise fulfilled!
hey, you got your wish!

trump's uncaged and unbound messenger pigeon post Capitol insurrection

twitter bird, you are
free now! he cannot hurt you
anymore! so there!

warning to my D.C. Black people on 1/6/2021

stand back and stand by
white boys are bringing their toys
Black folks, please stay home!

presidential record breaker
or
to boldly go where no POTUS has gone before

twice you've been impeached!
at least look at the bright side!
you won at something!

Binge Watching the Insurrectionist Arrests on YouTube

I get my thrills from
FBI busting them all!
Justice entertains.

Atlanta and Boulder
#nomorethoughtsandprayers

Two shootings, one week.
Hate's bullets never run out!
Gun reform right now!!!

trump insurrectionists, explain this to me...

Capitol insur-
rectionists always live in
parents' basements. Why?

Rationalization Much?

Colin kneels—you're mad???
Rioters are "patriots"?
Hey, sounds about White!

Cleaning Proud Boys' Mess

Shit and piss and blood
smeared on the Capitol walls!
Black and Brown folks cleaned!

rebutting conservative white folks' rebuttals post Capitol Hill insurrection

or

no buts, buts, or buts!

"but... but... ANTIFA!!!"
"but BLM torched portland!!!"

but five are dead now!

a few words on republican christian congressional enablers post Capitol insurrection

remember this–
evil says its prayers too.

recipe for slavery

preheat colonies to 1619 degrees.

pour heaping cups of africans into ships.
separate families and whip until bloody.
work into submission.
place into hot baking sun.

plate them up for your bidding.
enough africans to go around per master.

serves entire nation.

Thank You, Q

You are a walking poem that needs to be written.
Thanks for making my job that much easier.

You stole that buffalo headdress from a Native American.
Thanks, I guess, for caring enough to protect the muffins in the
 Capitol breakroom.

You claim you were on a divine pilgrimage to kill a vp and democracy.
Thanks to you, trump's fingerprints aren't on the murder weapon.

You are lucky that Supermax serves organic acai berries for breakfast
 every morning.
Thanks to your mom for making sure you eat right behind bars.

You do not have the right to walk our streets as a free man ever again.
Thanks, FBI, for reading him his rights!

SCAN ME

Putting Delta V on Notice

Hello, Miss Delta.
I know you're the new killer in town.
You burn up the young and unvaccinated like matchsticks.
You devour the meat of maskless Republicans and spit out the bones.
You bring nurses down to their knees in exhaustion and prayer.

Hear this—
I am not 21 and dumb.
I am not gullible or racist enough to believe Antifa or Asians cooked you up in some lab.
I am not adding my body to the clutter of COVID-filled bodies at a hospital.
Moreover, I refuse to wait a year or more to defend myself against a deadly spike pointed at me today.

You see, I've learned a lot in the 17 plus months since your evil twin 'Rona stepped foot in this town.
Long enough for me gather some chemical ammunition and disinfect you into oblivion.
Long enough for me to learn how to **FIGHT**!

I strap my armor on my face, ready for battle.
My stats speak for themselves—
Lynda 999, 'Rona 0.
The blood of the conquered drips from my fingertips and I wash it off for 20 seconds.

I may have been plagued in March 2020 but now I'm vaxed in August 2021.

You will never take me down.
I'm a poet who kills.

SCAN ME

To the Person Who Stole Mom's Lemon Tree During Lockdown

In the middle of a pandemic and you chose to steal
my mom's lemon tree–were you that desperate for a meal?
I get it, times are hard–food insecurity is real.
To your sense of decency, I'm trying to appeal!

It's a lemon, for God's sake–get your own at Trader Joe's!
Stand six feet apart and shop there–hope you got the memo!
If you don't wanna shop there, that's your problem, not mine, bro!
I want payback for the lemons you owe!

You're the one that doesn't wear a mask–I know who you are!
Today you steal lemons—what's next?? A car???

Breaking rules all over the place–that won't get you far!
Karmic retribution is scary–you'll be emotionally scarred!

Worked up about this issue much, Lynda? Kinda tearing you to bits?
What can I say? Quarantine's like a lemon—all sour and mostly pits!

SCAN ME

Lynda in the Affirmative (As of 2/21/2021)

I am still on lockdown eleven months later.
I am always busy in spite of sitting on my couch.
I am tired and stay up later than I should.

I am 57 and worried that I will never be married.
I am way too feminist to worry about my marital status.
I am actually shocked to mention that I am the above-mentioned
    age.
I am living proof that Black, indeed, does not crack.

I am glad trump isn't president any more.
I am scared that senatorial cowards have unleashed a monster post
    second impeachment.
I am witness to America falling apart but trying to come together.
I am a race woman in spite of modern White supremacy.

I am fighting every day against a virus that's an equal opportunity
    killer.
I am saddened that Black and Brown people have died under corona
    and racism's vicious knife.
I am alive in spite of all visible and invisible forces that want me
    dead.

I am the word conductor and letters are my notes.
I am listening to the Muse's music and singing her song.
I am a composer of 2020 and 2021, their melodies my words.

I am going strong.
I am not going ***ANYWHERE***.

SCAN ME

LYNDA LA ROSE is a poet/performance artist who has been writing since 1993. She has been published in several poetry anthologies including, *I Love Your Poetry, What?!?!, Listen to Me: Shared Secrets from WriteGirl, San Gabriel Poetry Calendar, and the City of Los Angeles African American Heritage Month Cultural Affairs Guide* for 2011, 2012 and 2013. Lynda wrote and performed her solo poetry/spoken word show, *Summerfruit* in 2007. In 2017, Lynda performed *Summerfruit* at the Hollywood Fringe Festival and it was a great success—two oversold nights and standing ovations on both nights! In 2018, Lynda performed an excerpt of *Summerfruit* at Bootleg Theatre's "Solo Queens Fest"—the show was well received with a standing ovation!

Lynda's writing is based on her own personal experiences and is a continuation of her self-expression and passion for language. She acted in several theatrical productions with the Walking Theatre Workshop in Venice, CA, and is currently creating video content of her poetry.

You can look Lynda up on her Facebook page, "Words that Whisper and Roar," Instagram at @lyndarosela, or www.lyndalarose.com. Lynda's ongoing collection of spoken word short films can be explored at www.YouTube.com/DelusionalDiva.

Made in the USA
Monee, IL
27 March 2023